How to Grow
FUCHSIAS

How to Grow
FUCHSIAS

Brian & Valerie Proudley

BLANDFORD PRESS
POOLE · DORSET

First published in the U.K. 1983 by Blandford Press, Link House, West Street, Poole, Dorset, BH15 1LL.

Copyright © 1983 Blandford Books Ltd.

Distributed in the United States by Sterling Publishing Co., Inc., 2 Park Avenue, New York, N.Y. 10016.

Adapted from material first published in FUCHSIAS IN COLOUR.

British Library Cataloguing in Publication Data

Proudley, Brian
How to grow fuchsias.
1. Fuchsias
I. Title   II. Proudley, Valerie
635.9'3344   SB413.F8

ISBN 0 7137 1376 3

Typeset in 9/11½pt Century Schoolbook by Poole Typesetting
Printed in Great Britain by R. J. Acford, Chichester

Contents

Introduction

Fashion is not confined entirely to the way in which we dress, for garden plants are as much controlled by fashion as are clothes. As today we see a revival in Edwardian or even Victorian modes of dress, so too can a renewed interest be seen in plants that were all the rage in those former times. The main difference between the two types of fashion is the speed with which changes occur. In *haute couture* the hemlines go up and down with familiar regularity, but in the garden changes take place at a much slower rate. Not all plants that were formerly held in high esteem make a comeback, for once the stock is lost they are gone for ever.

The Asiatic *Ranunculus* was one of the most prized of the old florist's flowers early in the nineteenth century, when almost one thousand different named sorts could be purchased. Fifty years later the numbers were down to a score, and today these formerly prized greenhouse gems are represented by just a handful, sold mostly in mixture. The double flowered exhibition hollyhock is another of the former florist plants that is no longer with us. Increased by cuttings only, these were named plants, unlike those of today that are raised from seed and sold too as a mixture or a strain. What of the fuchsia? The fuchsias so beloved of the elegant Edwardians could be put into the category of those plants that were formerly very popular and have now made a comeback. Many will not agree that this is strictly correct for they have been grown over the years, but we are speaking in general terms. One has only to look at the old catalogues to see the immense popularity these plants enjoyed in the late nineteenth century and up until World War I.

The present day popularity of the fuchsia is well known to all, but, unlike many of our better known garden plants, it does not have a very well documented early history. Gardening books, however, all agree that the honour of being the first to grow and sell fuchsias in Britain goes to the nursery firm of Lee and Kennedy. These grew the so called 'American Plants' at their nursery in Hammersmith, London, and were the first to flower the yellow *Rhododendron luteum* outside its natural habitat. Who better then to be the first to grow a true 'American Plant' – the fuchsia? How James Lee, one of the partners, got his first plant or plants is the subject of much controversy, for each account seems to differ slightly from the next. The most commonly told story is of how Lee heard of an unusual plant that was attracting considerable interest growing in a window in Wapping. At this time this was a small village to the north of London, and knowing of the public desire for something out of the ordinary he made his way there to visit the owner and judge the plant for himself. He learned that it had been given to the lady of the house by a relative, a seaman recently returned from South America. Some bargaining is said to have taken place before money changed hands and the plant was borne back to the nursery, there to receive the attentions of the propagator. If this sounds something like a fairy tale that is because it probably is!

Another version has it that James Lee obtained cuttings of *F. coccinea* from the Royal Gardens at Kew, albeit 'deviously'. We know that they had a single plant of this species in one of the greenhouses, for it is recorded in *Botanical Magazine* of 1789 that a Captain Firth had brought back a plant from Brazil and presented it to them the previous year. This fact is also mentioned in Aiton's *Hortus Kewensis.* Yet another version links the two stories by stating that it was Captain Firth's wife who sold the plant to the nurseryman. We suppose that if he had brought back several plants it would provide a simple answer. What is

8

certain is that to have built up a stock of some three hundred plants in the five years before they came on the market would not have been difficult. The cost of the specimen in the first story we do not know, although the offspring fetched 'not less than a guinea, up to ten guineas according to size'.

The generic name *Fuchsia* had been coined nearly one hundred years earlier by Père Charles (or Carolo in Latin) Plumier, a French Jesuit monk. He discovered the plant known today as *F. triphylla* growing in the mountains of Santo Domingo (Dominican Republic). Père Plumier was a Minim, a member of a mendicant order in which the brothers owned no personal property but relied on charity as well as working for their existence. Born in Marseilles in the year 1646, he was admitted to the order when he was sixteen. He laboured as a wood turner, writing a book on the subject based on his practical experience. The study of mathematics was another of his interests and he took up botany as a relief from his other work. It was his great love of plants of all kinds that was eventually to take him to the Americas no less then three times, an arduous journey in those days. In the capacity of Royal Botanist to Louis XIV of France, he was searching for plants of economic importance.

Descriptions des Plantes de l'Amerique, his first botanical work, appeared in 1695 after his first journey. More interesting to us is *Nova Plantarum Americanarum Genera*, produced after his third voyage and published in Paris in 1703, for in it the name *Fuchsia* appears for the very first time.

Some fifty people connected with botany in some way are commemorated in this work by having their names formed into generic designations. The name *Fuchsia* was a compliment to Leonhart Fuchs, a German doctor of medicine who as well as being eminent in this field was also a capable botanist, for the two subjects were closely linked. Sad to say he was never to know that such an important and beautiful group of plants was named in his honour, for he died in 1566 many years before the discovery of the plant that bears his name.

The reason that Dr Fuchs was known to Père Plumier was the

existence of Fuchs' own book *De Historia Stirpium.* Published at Basle in 1542, it contained some remarkably accurate wood-cuts of wild flowers, including a plate of the Common Spotted Orchis *Dactylorhiza fuchsii.* Its present specific epithet (the name that differentiates between species in the same genus) also commemorates the doctor.

Latin is the language used today by botanists to describe new species. Writers in former times not only used Latin for the text of the books but for their own names as well. Fuchs was no exception to the custom: although he did not translate his name altogether, he did change it to Fuchsius, which is very similar to the names, both Latin and common, of the plant under discussion.

Plumier's drawings and text describing his finds went to the great naturalist Linnaeus who included the genus *Fuchsia* in his monumental work *Species Plantarum.* Plumier called his plant *Fuchsia triphylla, flore coccineo,* there being nothing unusual in a name of that length at the time. Plant names were a short description – this one means simply three-leaved scarlet-flowered fuchsia. In his book, Linnaeus, using his binomial method of presenting the name of a plant for the first time, omitted the last part of Plumier's name.

Was *Fuchsia triphylla* brought into cultivation when first discovered? There is no reason to suggest that it was not, but when no economic use was discovered it would probably have been discarded. In fact, so inaccurate were the drawings in Plumier's book that many doubted for several years the existence of the species described. Although obviously a fuchsia of some kind, *F. triphylla* was not rediscovered until 1872 in the same island where Plumier was said to have found the first.

Nurseryman James Lee started selling his plants of *F. coccinea* in 1793. So successful were they that the nurserymen who had purchased the originals, seeing the public interest, eagerly acquired new species as they arrived from South America. This was the golden age of the plant collector. If certain plants were wanted, collectors were soon despatched to find them and before long hybrids between the species appeared. All of these very early hybrids have disappeared, but a seedling cultivar that was raised by a Mr Gulliver who was the gardener to the Reverend S. Marriot of Horsmonden could be obtained comparatively recently, and may be growing in a greenhouse somewhere still. Named 'Venus-Victrix' it was a landmark in its day, as it was the first to bear almost white sepals and tube with a contrasting bright purple corolla. Although nothing much when judged by today's standards, it was well received when introduced by Cripps the nurserymen of nearby Tunbridge Wells. Of importance too is the role that this small flowered chance seedling has had in the production of new and better cultivars, for the white sepals and tube present in many of today's cultivars have most probably carried through the years since 'Venus-Victrix' first appeared.

The cultivation of the fuchsia was by no means confined to Britain, for in 1848 a notable book appeared in France entitled *Le Fuchsia: son Histoire et sa Culture.* Written by Felix Porcher, it included a list of some five hundred and twenty species, hybrids and cultivars. We know today that many of these were in fact duplicates. This is not surprising, for as plants from abroad received French names confusion reigned when the plants sent to Britain were sometimes sent back under a third name. The publication of such a work does however give an insight into the tremendous popularity and success gained in the few years since hybridisation first started.

The nursery firm of Lemoine from Nancy, France, were one of the best known continental raisers and growers. They produced in the years from 1850 to World War I some splendid cultivars many of which figure prominently in today's catalogues: 'Princess Dollar', 'Brutus' and 'Molesworth' amongst others.

Of the British growers, the firm of Veitch deserves a mention, for they were instrumental in promoting many new plants, both species and hybrids. Their collector, William Lobb, travelled extensively in both North and South America, sending back seeds of several important subjects. He is known best of all for

11

his introduction of the 'Wellingtonia' tree *Sequoiadendron giganteum* into Britain, but an earlier find was a plant that Veitch's flowered for the first time in 1847 and called *Fuchsia spectabilis* (it was probably *F. denticulata*). It was found by Lobb in 1844 on his first journey to South America where he also collected large quantities of 'Monkey Puzzle' *Araucaria araucana*, another plant so beloved of the Victorians.

Story's were a nursery firm based at Newton Abbot, Devon. They were the first to breed a fuchsia with double flowers and also the first to bring out those with a pure white corolla in both single and double forms. One of their best known introductions at that time was 'Queen Victoria'. One of several plants with the same name, it no doubt proved popular with the subjects of the then reigning monarch.

By now there were in existence both a plant with white sepals and tube and also one having a white corolla. The next logical step would seem to be a cross between these two to procure a completely white bloom, but plant breeding is not that simple. An almost complete knowledge of the ancestry of each parent as well as a knowledge of the workings of genetics is required before the hybridist can predict the likely outcome of his labours. No such information appears to have been used and for the workers who attempted the early crosses the pure white bloom must have seemed as remote as the rose fancier's elusive pure blue rose. It seems to be human nature to strive after something which appears to be impossible. Not until comparatively recently has this dream become reality. The next goal is a deep yellow large-flowered hybrid.

During the last century the art of cultivating the fuchsia reached a very high level indeed, and fuchsias were grown on a scale that will probably never be seen again. Greenhouses were filled, others graced conservatories, many were grown as bedding. Few were the great houses of the time that could not boast of a notable collection. Many kept a gardener whose sole duty it was to care for the plants, training them into columns, standards, espaliers and pyramids. In suburban villas they were used for bedding out as well as indoors and many thousands were produced annually for the purpose. These were raised in the vineries that ringed London where fuchsias were treated as a 'catch crop' to be sold before the vine foliage got too dense in summer. The metropolis has now spread out to swallow up the land where many of these glasshouses stood, but many of the plants they housed are still with us. 'Ballet Girl', 'Display' and 'Mrs Rundle' are some of the tough, free-branching sorts that were grown for the market trade as it was termed.

The coming of World War I brought great changes to every way of life. Gardens were especially hard hit. With the shortage of staff to care for the flowers the poor fuchsia was ousted from the greenhouses to make way for something more mundane – the tomato. The decline in general popularity had begun. With the war over it is difficult to see why an immediate renewal in interest did not take place, but it did not.

How was it that our plant was so soon forgotten when a few short years before it had been all the rage? It has been suggested that a rebellion against anything Victorian was the cause. In the new modern world of the early 1920s the fuchsia, the tiny red and purple flowered sorts in particular, certainly comes into this category. Even today few plants can conjure up a better picture of the Victorian era. The breaking up of the large estates brought about changes in gardening methods unthought of previously, but a more likely reason for the fuchsia's decline is that many fuchsias had become extinct after being turned out of their warm shelter. This was the dawning of the age of the home gardener (as distinct from the cottager). The home gardener with memories of the magnificent specimens formerly to be seen at exhibitions and flower shows could not for a moment believe that they would grow under less than ideal conditions. Thus to the general public our plant remained in the doldrums for several years. Admittedly, they could be seen in public parks where neat formal bedding schemes often featured fuchsias. Several of the hardy kinds had already become established garden plants prior to this time, growing in the shrubbery or on the rock garden. Who has not

13

seen the magnificent flowering hedges of fuchsias in the West Country, Devon, Cornwall, Wales and Scotland or marvelled at the vigour and cascading wealth of flower of these naturalised plants? Squeezing the buds to make them 'pop' will often be among people's earliest childhood memories. The cottage garden became a home for many of the favourites, while specialists have since found old, scarce sorts still flourishing in their refuge.

To pinpoint a general revival in interest is not easy as it has been so gradual. By the early 1930s fuchsias were once again being planted. A few years earlier in 1928 the American Fuchsia Society was formed. It is inevitable that when sufficient people have a particular interest in one plant specialist societies will be started. The fuchsia is no exception, for there are today societies flourishing around the world with a total membership running into several thousands. Being a member of such a group is of great value to novice and expert alike. The former will receive all the assistance required in the various aspects of cultivation, whilst the more experienced gains from the up-to-date knowledge disseminated from other growers through the society. In the United States there are two large organisations, the American Fuchsia Society and the National Fuchsia Society, as well as many smaller groups. Enthusiasts in other parts of the world are in turn well catered for with a specialist society (see pp. 89–91). Britain too has its own with members and affiliated groups all over the kingdom.

Some fifty different fuchsia cultivars collected in Britain by Professor S. B. Mitchell were distributed to growers in California, both commercial and amateur, soon after the founding of the American Fuchsia Society, and they have played a part in the breeding programmer of the raisers there. The magnificent progeny of those introductions made their debut in Britain at the flower shows in the early 1950s. The fact that such creations can, despite their delicate appearance, tolerate not only the perils of an English summer, but in some cases the rigours of a winter too, never ceases to amaze. Do not assume, however, that all modern fuchsias can be attempted year-round in a cold climate; several are not hardy, others display their flowers better with protection. The heads and stems of standards will not survive except in the really favoured parts. Nevertheless, there is available today a range of types, colours and forms with a vigour that puts some of the older cultivars in the shade. The hybridists in America and Britain, as well as other countries, are still busy producing variations. Sports occur occasionally too, to swell the numbers of good things to be grown, each year seeing the introduction of several new sorts. There seems to be no end to the number and it is difficult to know or anticipate just what is likely to be seen in the years ahead. Because something is new it does not necessarily follow that it is better. That is why many of the old tried and trusted sorts are still planted, so as well as being the forebears of the modern plants they too still have a valuable place in the garden.

For the fuchsia the future looks promising for there are few flowering shrubs with the ability to give such a return for the relatively small amount of cultural effort needed. They produce a wealth of colour whether grown in pots in the greenhouse or outdoors in the border or rockery, as climbers against a wall, decorating a loggia, in hanging baskets, or as house plants. All flower profusely in sun or shade.

1
Nomenclature

What is the difference between a variety and a cultivar? What is a species? These are the sort of questions that newcomers to gardening frequently ask. Although the answers will probably not enable one to grow better fuchsias, knowing the origin of the name gives added interest.

A species is the lowest basic unit on which the classification of all biology is founded. Two fuchsias of the same species will reproduce themselves exactly when, after cross-pollination, the resultant seedlings appear. Several species having only slight differences are formed together into a genus. Groups of genera (plural of genus) with general similarities are arranged into Families or Natural Orders.

Fuchsia is a genus within the Natural Order Onagraceae which anyone interested in wild flowers will recognise as the willow-herb family. This numbers among its members the familiar garden plants *Godetia, Clarkia* and the evening primrose *Oenothera*, weeds such as that pretty but troublesome invader of shady parts of the garden, Enchanter's nightshade *Circaea*, and also the willow-herbs themselves, some of which are weeds, but many of which are attractive wild flowers. These are all related to the fuchsia.

Two species within the same genus are sometimes capable of producing a hybrid when cross-pollinated, natural hybrids often occurring in the wild; intermediate in character between their parents, many make good garden plants. Natural hybrids can receive a cultivar name, but only when brought into cultivation. Hybridists using two, three or even more species back-cross seedlings with a parent. Once a desired offspring has come about, this too can receive such a name, after being propagated. Another way in which a new cultivar can come about is when a plant sports or mutates, giving rise to a branch or shoot that differs materially from the original. Several extremely good fuchsias originated in this manner, including all the coloured foliage forms.

What is the difference between a cultivar (cv or cvs in the plural) and a variety? The word variety was once, and still is for that matter, used to describe a cultivated plant that is now correctly known as a cultivar. Confusion can come about when using variety for these garden plants as it is the word that botanists use for a naturally occurring geographical form of a species. In *Fuchsia* this happens with *F. magellanica* in particular as we shall see later. These plants are not distinct enough to warrant the rank of a separate specific name and they are capable of interbreeding freely with the type. The Latin designation for them is *varietas,* always abbreviated in the name to *var.*

In some large genera there are groups of species which resemble one another more closely than others in the same genus. These are formed into series or sections with each section having a 'type plant' which is regarded as the most typical of the group. The genus *Fuchsia* is so arranged with seven sections. One of these, Eufuchsia, with fifty-eight species, is by far the largest, the other extreme being Kierschlegeria with *F. lycioides* as the single representative.

Here are some typical fuchsia names:

1 *Fuchsia*	*magellanica*	var. *molinae*	Section Quelusia
Genus	species	subspecies	Section in genus

This is a wild plant but also in cultivation in an identical form.

2 *Fuchsia* x *bacillaris*
  Genus   Hybrid

The x shows that this is a hybrid or cross between two species within the same genus. It may be a wild plant or may come about in cultivation.

3 *Fuchsia* 'Enfant Prodigue' ('Prodigy') LEMOINE 1887 French
  Genus   Cultivar   Synonym Raiser Date Country

The name between the single quotes is that of a 'man-made' plant which is in cultivation only and is never found in the wild. Nearly all the fuchsias we grow fall into this group. A synonym is another name for the same plant (the example quoted is a mistranslation of *enfant prodigue,* 'prodigal child').

The compilation of the correct names of any genus as large as *Fuchsia* involves a great amount of research both in the field, in herbaria and often in the laboratory too. Anyone interested in our subject should be grateful to Dr Philip Munz for his work *A Revision of the Genus Fuchsia (Onagraceae),* first published in 1943 by the California Academy of Sciences. Although basically a scientific work, it is of immense value to the keen fuchsia grower, for in it he not only revises the nomenclature of the genus as a whole, but also sets out the classification as we know it today, bringing order out of confusion in a masterly way.

With the introduction of species taking place over several years, it is not always easy to be certain whether a plant is really new to science or horticulture, or simply a re-introduction. Nurserymen have usually been the recipients of seeds sent back by collectors. In many cases they have not had the means of knowing whether or not they have been introduced previously. Several fuchsias have received synonyms in the past for this reason.

The naming of wild plants (species) is now in accordance with the 'International Code of Botanical Nomenclature'. The 'Rule of Priority', i.e. the use of the earliest given name for a plant, which has meant name changes for many fuchsias in the past,

18

appears now to have more or less stabilised the names. The 'International Code of Nomenclature for Cultivated Plants', as its name suggests, governs all the names for plants we grow in our gardens. New cultivars of fuchsias are now subject to the code before acceptance. Briefly, the name should be new and not the same as one given previously, even though the original plant has been lost. The suffix 'improved' is frowned on, as is the generic name of another plant, e.g. *Fuchsia* 'Erica' is disallowed but *Fuchsia* 'Heather' is all right. The name can be in any language capable of being printed in Roman type, but not in Latin which is reserved for the names of wild plants. Many fuchsias have names which, because they were given prior to the introduction of the code, must still be used although today they would not comply.

The more important groups of garden plants have a specialist body to which application for the registration of a new name has to be addressed. In our case it is to the American Fuchsia Society, who since 1967, have had the responsibility of checking names as a safeguard against duplication. They also vet new names to see that they comply with the code.

How many fuchsias have been named in the past? This is a difficult question to answer. One estimate puts the figure at around five thousand. This may sound exaggerated, but, if anything, we think it is an underestimate. Fuchsias lend themselves to hybridisation readily and although not all introductions are winners for obvious reasons, good new cultivars are eagerly sought to join the ranks of established favourites.

Except for a few species cultivated in Britain in greenhouses only, most of the fuchsias we grow today are descended from hybrids resulting from early crosses between two or more species with *F. magellanica, fulgens, coccinea,* and later *triphylla* and others playing the role of seed or pollen parent. To trace the complete ancestry of the modern plant is impossible owing to the very considerable amount of breeding that has taken place, but in some there are features that give a clue to their forebears. The so called 'Triphylla Hybrids' with their distinctive flower shape give a good indication even if the parent were unknown. *F. magellanica* has imparted a great deal of hardiness to its offspring thus making fuchsias more popular than if they were only confined to the greenhouse. Only found in the New World, the genus *Fuchsia* forms part of the indigenous flora of Central and South America occurring down the Pacific seaboard from Mexico to Chile, as well as in other countries in the continent. The West Indies, New Zealand and Tahiti are other countries in which some species are found growing as wild plants. They are almost all found in mountainous areas, some at a great height growing in situations where the plants are subjected to a considerable amount of rain or cloud-borne mist. Those types that make their home in the dense rain forests of South America also grow in conditions of high humidity. The ability not only to survive under these conditions but to revel in them must be remembered in hot dry situations. The foliage needs to be kept crisp and turgid if the plants are not to suffer. Shade from the hot sun, syringing the foliage with clean water, and use a compost that does not dry out when the pots are left unattended for a while. Planted out in the soil the fuchsias are less likely to suffer once established, but even here a gentle spray in the cool of the evening is always appreciated.

Wild fuchsias range in size from low creeping plants up to fairly large shrubs or even small trees. Some are epiphytes, others vine-like climbers creeping up tall trees in a manner far removed from the popular notion of how a fuchsia should grow.

The flowers are produced from the leaf axils and are in the form of a tube-like calyx which is split at the open end into four sepals. It is interesting to note that all wild members of the Onagraceae have the parts of the flower in fours, or a constant multiple of that number. The corolla of the fuchsia consists of four petals in most species, although in at least one, *F. apetala*, they are absent. The dainty flowers are carried on a slender pedicel, or stalk; in the garden plants they are produced mainly in pairs but in the species they may be in clusters or a fairly large raceme.

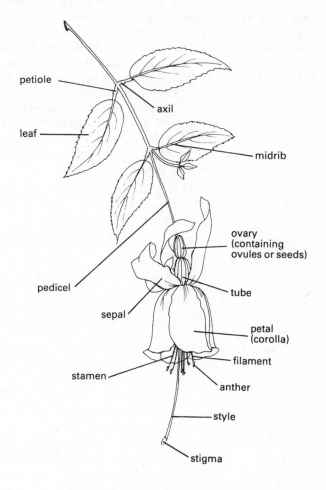

petiole

axil

leaf

midrib

ovary
(containing
ovules or seeds)

pedicel

tube

sepal

petal
(corolla)

filament

stamen

anther

style

stigma

Parts of the fuchsia flower and stem.

There are eight (rarely four) very noticeable stamens, each filament carrying its pollen-bearing anther, with the female parts – stigma, style and ovary – completing the flower. Unlike that of many plants, the reproductive mechanism is very prominent, adding considerably to the beauty and charm of the flower, in some cases the actual colour enhancing the shade of the more decorative part. The fertilised seeds are contained in the four part ovary at the base of the tube or calyx (tube and sepals). When the flower has dropped the ovary develops into a fleshy edible berry, rather insipid to the taste. In the wild these berries are avidly devoured by birds, by which means, after passing through, the seeds are distributed.

2
Ordering and Caring for Young Plants

Several species of *Fuchsia* have been involved in the evolution or development of the plants we grow today. Not that this need concern us too much regarding the actual cultivation, but it does have a bearing on hardiness. Some are almost completely hardy, to be kept in the garden throughout the year as permanent subjects. Others need year-round greenhouse protection, or in those countries fortunate enough not to be subject to frosts the use of a lath or shade house to protect from sun and wind. The bulk of our modern plants, however, fall between the two extremes, flourishing in the open garden during the summer but demanding warm winter quarters in cold countries, including Britain. Even here, within this last group, are many that are hardier than is generally realised, which will usually come through an average winter with only the minimum of protection. Most are so quick in growth that it is perfectly feasible to purchase strong plants in late spring, enjoy a superb display all summer, then simply discard them when cold weather ends the flowering. They are cheap enough to buy so that many find it easier to do this each season, thus avoiding the bother associated with storing the dormant plants. Of course, the results from older second and third year plants can be better, so we are not advocating renewing each season if space is available to store.

The selection of the fuchsias that are to be grown is made long before the plants are actually wanted. This is done by choosing either directly from a nurseryman's catalogue or from a list of favourites noted the previous summer. There is no better way of making a choice than to see the plants growing, rather than depending on a description in a price list. Try to visit one of the major flower shows. The leading specialists who exhibit at the larger shows are only too pleased to give helpful advice to intending purchasers and others. The Botanic Gardens usually keep an up-to-date collection, together with many of the older kinds and species too. Bearing in mind the varying uses for the plants, get the list off to the nurseryman as early in the season as possible. This will assist by helping him plan his likely needs of each particular sort. Those leaving their ordering to the last moment may be disappointed to find that certain kinds are not available. You should state with the order the approximate time when you will be in a position to take the plants. Remember, they will have been grown in warm conditions and will need a similar temperature after arrival. Where heating is not installed in greenhouse or frame, it may be more prudent to delay delivery until the days (and nights) warm up a little, then just sufficient heat to keep out frost will be acceptable.

Collecting the young plants from a nursery is always best but if this is inconvenient or not possible, express delivery will ensure safe arrival. Unpack them carefully as soon as they are delivered, repotting into a pot of the size of the root ball, except where the compost differs materially from your own. In that case, it is better to remove most of it with much care and to treat the young plants as large rooted cuttings. The roots of plants growing in a soilless compost often show a marked reluctance to leave their little ball of peat and difficulty is sometimes experienced over the even distribution of water in the pot unless a similar compost is being used. Keep the atmosphere close by dampening down paths and staging for several days until plants have recovered from the move. Some people shade pots to assist in this, particularly when the young plants have been several days in transit; light syringing over the foliage early in the morning well before the sun has much heat will help at this time.

The secret of success with fuchsias, especially during the growing on period, is to keep them moving without a check. This will mean a larger pot as soon as the first becomes filled with roots. One thing they dislike is to be over-potted (using too large a pot for each move which allows the surplus compost to become sour). A 3 in (8 cm) pot should be exchanged for a 5 in (13 cm) pot, then for a 7 in (18 cm) pot (for a specimen). Many plants will go through the first season in the intermediate size, but older, larger plants are often put into 12 in (30 cm) pots or tubs for the subsequent years. If potting-on is done at the right time the root-ball, with the exception of any drainage crocks in the base, can be left intact after each move.

In his fascinating book *Familiar Garden Flowers,* published about 1890, the writer, the Reverend Shirley Hibberd, passes on the advice given him to grow fuchsias as if they were radishes. It may sound a little absurd to compare the two, but anyone who relishes them will know that the best radishes are produced in a warm mellow soil constantly moist but completely without stagnation. These conditions are exactly the same as the young fuchsia enjoys.

Fresh compost for the roots at each stage in the potting-on will result in production of stems and foliage at the expense of flowers. As fuchsias flower at the season when the days are long, the answer is to get through the initial growing period quickly during the early part of the year so that plants are in their final pots for the season and one can enjoy plentiful bloom as the days lengthen.

Composts

We mix our own composts, as do many growers, both amateur and professional. Over the years some quite weird concoctions have been advocated but although we make our own we keep to the formulae worked out by Messrs Lawrence and Newall of the John Innes Horticultural Institute (J. I. Composts). There are five composts – one for seedlings, four for potting. They vary from fine (J. I. seed) which we also use for rooting cuttings, to fairly coarse for potting (Nos 1, 2, 3 and 4). The potting composts differ only in the amount of fertilisers added, most growers regarding No. 2 as the best for fuchsias.

Some of the newer peat-based composts are excellent once the technique of using them has been mastered. The University of California (U. C.) have done considerable research in this field and have produced formulae to suit most plants, including fuchsias.

Ready-mixed composts

Potting composts can normally be obtained mixed ready for use. When bought in bags, the material should be neither too fresh nor too old before use. Many of these composts when first mixed give off gases harmful to tender roots owing to the fertilising element present. Others contain resin-coated fertiliser which does not start working until the material has been moistened. Should the compost prove fresh it will be advisable to turn the bag out onto a hard floor surface (under cover) turning the pile at least twice at intervals of several days before using. In old compost the danger lies in the build-up of salts in the material; chlorosis (yellowing of the foliage, damage or even death of tender roots) can often be traced to compost mixed many months before. Compost three months old should be safe; after that it is doubtful. We would be wary of compost mixed the previous season, which is sometimes offered for sale.

Ready-mixed, the compost may be formulated in two completely different ways: loam-based or soilless. Loam-based means that the material contains a proportion of good loam, together with peat to provide humus for moisture retention and sand to keep the mixture 'open' or aerated allowing surplus water to drain quickly through. A balanced fertiliser is incorporated to maintain growth for several months. The most frequently produced are those made up to the J. I. formulae which in our opinion are the best for all-round amateur use.

Making up compost at home

When suitable materials are obtainable, composts of high quality can be made up at home. This involves a little more effort maybe, but it is often better than the purchased article and considerably cheaper, which is worth considering when perhaps there are a hundred large pots to fill! Loam, which for preference should be slightly greasy, is obtained by rotting down very thick turves cut from an old pasture. These are laid grass-side down in a stack, to be left for six months or a year before screening or shredding to remove stones and coarse material. Sterilising by heat can be done at this time, or alternatively with chemicals well in advance of the time of use. Not all growers sterilise compost for the growing of fuchsias, but as it is standard nursery practice we prefer to do it, for not only soil-borne diseases are killed but weed seeds as well. The rough material left after screening can be put to one side for use as drainage (we call this roughage) in the bottom of the larger pots.

The next ingredient is peat; granulated sphagnum moss peat is best. It usually comes in large bales which do not require sterilising, and it is virtually weed-free. Dry peat should be well soaked and allowed to drain before it is used; the easiest way to tackle this is to turn out the bale onto a level concrete area, make a well in the centre of the pile and fill with water. Sprinkle dry peat into this until all the water is absorbed. Turn the whole lot over, repeating the process until all is saturated. Leave the mixture to 'bulk' or swell for a few days, allowing it to drain completely before use. Leafmould can be used as a substitute or an alternative to peat. It should be treated to neutralise harmful organisms. The most satisfactory material to use is that obtained by gathering the fallen leaves of oak or beech and stacking them neatly for a year or more until they are of a light crumbly texture. Bracken foliage in a partly rotted state is excellent for fuchsias when it can be found in sufficient quantity. Both these materials will require screening before use; the coarse waste should be retained for use in the base of large size pots.

Sand comes in many forms from ground rock to volcanic

scoria. The origin is not important as long as it is clean, coarse, free from lime or other minerals. Soft pit sand with dust-like particles as used in the building trade is unsuitable, but their sharp sand is often perfectly usable. Most garden centres stock good quality horticultural sand. To facilitate mixing, use sand in as dry a state as possible. The feeding element is added by incorporating a mixture of fertilisers (except for the seed mix). For J. I. compost there is a ready-made formulation known as J. I. base. It can be purchased in Britain or made up using separate materials (see below).

Assemble all the materials and measure the total to determine the quantity of fertiliser required. A standard measuring box can be made either from suitable pieces of timber or from an existing box converted to a rectangle with the dimensions 12 × 12 × 15 in (30 × 30 × 40 cm). This will hold about 36 litres or one bushel (British – the American bushel is slightly smaller). The weighed quantity of fertiliser can now be sprinkled on the top of the pile which is then mixed by turning completely at least three times. To ensure the even distribution of the fertiliser this can be mixed with the sand before it is added to the pile of loam and peat.

Formulae for composts

J. I. SEED For raising seedlings, rooting cuttings and first potting.

By bulk:

2 parts loam (passed through a fine sieve)

1 part peat (moist, medium or fine grade)

1 part sand (dry)

To each measure add 56 g (2 oz) superphosphate of lime.

Note: The small amount of superphosphate required per bushel, although not critical, is not easy to measure. In practice one would probably mix a minimum of 5 bushels at one time thus bringing the weight up to a more reasonable amount to handle.

J. I. 2 For potting-on.

By bulk:

7 parts loam (passed through a medium sieve)

3 parts peat (moist, medium grade)

2 parts sand (dry, coarse)

To each bushel measure add 112 g (4 oz) J. I. Base or slow-release general fertiliser. Some growers advocate a larger quantity of fertiliser than this. Our own experience suggests that using a lower initial amount but continuing liquid feeding as soon as the plants are established in their pots gives the best results.

JOHN INNES BASE FERTILISER Where J. I. base is unobtainable the same mixture can be made from the following:

By bulk:

2 parts superphosphate of lime

2 parts hoof and horn (ground)

1 part sulphate of potash

Many report good results from the more recent slow release general fertilisers when used in place of J. I. base. These balanced materials have the added bonus of a wide spectrum of the trace elements which are so vital for plant growth. In loam-based composts made to the J. I. formulae these should already be present provided that the loam is of good quality.

Acidity

It is to be preferred if the compost has a slightly acid reaction when used for growing fuchsias. For this reason the chalk which is a vital part of the standard type of J. I. composts can be omitted when making up whether the loam contains lime or not. Should the loam prove to be slightly alkaline (containing free lime) it can still be used for compost making if corrected. To render loam acid, flowers of sulphur should be incorporated in the mix. The rate at which this is used will depend on the pH of the loam. Try 50 g (about $1\frac{1}{2}$ oz) per bushel measure: if the compost is still not acid the value of the loam for growing fuchsias is in doubt. An alternative method for correcting a compost and thus releasing essential plant foods is to water the plants after each repotting with an iron chelate such as 'Sequestrene'®. Used at the manufacturer's suggested strength it will also counter the effect of hard tap water used in watering. When liquid feed is given, this too will neutralise the lime which comes in via the tap, as it is slightly acid.

Treatment of prepared compost

After mixing, keep the prepared compost under cover, turning once or twice before using to aerate the material and disperse any toxic gases present. Do not use for two weeks after mixing or keep for longer than three to four months. The compost when used should be sufficiently moist to retain its shape after squeezing in the hand, yet it should break down easily when pressed with the thumb.

Soilless compost

Owing to the difficulty experienced around the globe in obtaining regular supplies of good quality loam and the variable nature of the material, several composts have been developed using peat and sand with added nutrients. Much of the pioneer work in this field was done at the University of California; their composts are known as the U. C. composts. Since the publication of the results of their experiments, many proprietary mixes have come into the market based broadly on their ideas. The main differences between these newer formulations and the traditional types which, incidentally, they have replaced in the majority of commercial establishments, are as follows:

1) *Weight.* Generally speaking they are considerably lighter. This is fine when large pots have to be moved but they easily fall over when the plants grow large!

2) *Nutrition.* They are lower in initial nutrient content which means that feeding must be started earlier.

3) *Watering.* The aim when watering must be to avoid over- or under-watering. In a peat-based compost this is far more critical

than when a loam-based one is used. Allowing the medium to become too dry will result in the peat shrinking from the sides of the pot so that a complete immersion is needed to re-wet the compost. On the other hand if the compost is allowed to become too wet, as sometimes happens in dull weather, it may prove difficult to manage as it will take some time to get back to normal. A wet compost means that aeration is affected, a state of affairs in which the roots start to rot in extreme cases. Now that we have said all that let us hasten to add that these comments are by no means intended to dissuade anyone from trying these materials, but to point out some of the pitfalls to be avoided.

Formula for soilless compost

Apart from the ready-mixed composts that are offered for sale it is possible to make up a good mixture at home using readily available materials.

Soilless compost for potting-on
   By bulk:
   1 part peat (moist, fine grade)
   1 part sand(dry, good quality horticultural)
To each bushel measure add
   By weight:
   56 g (2 oz) J. I. base or slow release general fertiliser
   56 g (2 oz) ground chalk
   56 g (2 oz) dolomitic limestone (magnesian limestone)
     (crushed)
Note The incorporation of lime in these forms is essential to pre-vent the build-up of acid salts.
For rooting cuttings use the above but without the fertiliser.

Pots

The choice of pots or containers is a personal one. Some stand by the traditional clay but more use the newer plastic types. Clay pots have the advantage that they are porous, so that over-watering is less likely, although this itself leads to greater demands for attention during hot, dry weather. New clay pots should be soaked overnight and allowed to dry again before using. After firing at very high temperature during manufacture it will be found that they absorb a considerable amount of water when immersed. Watering in the normal way is insufficient to make the pots usable and any advantage of porosity is lost; the same can apply to pots that are painted either inside or out.

How to 'crock' a pot to provide adequate drainage.

Previously used pots, whether clay or plastic, should always be scrubbed clean and dried before use. Drainage can be provided by placing pieces of broken pot in the base of the selected container (polystyrene foam broken into small chunks is a good alternative). We use the rough material left after screening the loam but take out the stones.

Watering

When correctly made, J. I. 2 compost has a sharp 'open' texture that is free draining. Even so to be safe we advocate the use of additional drainage material, for fuchsias detest a soggy medium. The expert keeps the compost on the dry side when the plants are young, maintaining growth by frequent syringing of the foliage. Watering should be a good soak, then the plant should be allowed almost to dry out. Do not be tempted, as some are, to give a little, often, as this invariably leads to dry parts occurring in the pot. An occasional dunking of the pot, plant as well, will do much good as long as it is in full growth (but not

Dunking both pot and plant can be beneficial.

flowering!) and drainage is adequately provided for. Leave the pot under the water until air bubbles cease to rise. The foliage which is rinsed at the same time is cleared of the odd insects that have escaped the sprayer. Most problems associated with watering a collection can be overcome by *a)* keeping to one compost, *b)* not mixing different types of pot.

Preparing young plants for the garden

There should be enough feeding present in J. I. 2 for those plants destined for summer bedding without anything additional being required. For outdoor work in Britain and Europe the shorter growing self-branching kinds are best as these require the minimum of staking. Before planting out they must be gradually hardened by placing them out of doors during daylight and returning them to shelter at night; in a short while the plants become acclimatised and can remain out at night. Wait until the danger from late frost is past before planting out in the position they are to occupy for the summer or permanently as the case may be. It sometimes happens that the shock of moving from the moist air of the greenhouse results in the loss of some of the foliage but this is replaced as new shoots appear from the leaf axils and should not affect the flowering.

3
Growing Fuchsias in the Garden

When fuchsias are to be grown in the garden, the choice will be between planting out the hardy types permanently or treating them as summer bedding, in which case they are put in when frosts have ceased in the spring, to be removed after flowering has finished in the autumn. For permanent planting (this also applies to countries where frosts are not prevalent) the position in which they are sited is going to have a considerable bearing on success. Drying wind is to be avoided wherever possible, for under these conditions far too much moisture evaporates from the foliage to the detriment of the plant.

It is not easy to lay down hard and fast rules for siting the border, for fuchsias are individuals when it comes to their likes and dislikes. In general, the paler colours are better when planted out of the full glare of the sun whereas the deeper shades tolerate it better without spoiling. A bed that gains shelter from a fence or wall can be utilised in exposed places; a hedge too is useful to break the wind's force. In a windy spot without much shelter the shorter, more compact types can be selected. Try to position these where they can gain some shelter from taller subjects. The main consideration after shelter from drying wind is to see that they have a moist yet free-draining soil, well provided with humus. Although the hardy fuchsias will grow perfectly well in ordinary garden soil, it will soon become apparent when care has been taken in its preparation. Better foliage, flowers in greater abundance, better colour, a more vigorous plant more able to come through the cold season unharmed – these are the rewards for diligence in this aspect of cultivation.

Preparing the site

We must assume here that the reader has a basic knowledge of gardening, is capable of digging, removing all perennial weeds etc. without further instruction. Where vacant ground is to be used for the planting, a start can be made in the autumn. To give of its best the fuchsia needs a cool deep root-run, so, in light or

Preparing a bed for planting. Break up the subsoil (left) and then add humus and mix in (right).

heavy soils, plenty of humus-forming material must be incorporated. This can be in the form of well-rotted farmyard manure (FYM), peat, leafmould, compost (garden variety), spent hops, wool shoddy (old rags make a good substitute!), anything in fact that will assist in the water retention when rotted down into humus. Even so, artificial means of watering may have to be resorted to in a prolonged dry spell.

Beds should be trenched, the sub-soil well broken with a fork before spreading the source of humus along the bottom and mixing in. Heavy wet ground will benefit from extra drainage which you can provide by mixing in sand or weathered ashes.

Do fuchsias need an acid or limy soil? The ideal pH, as the scale to determine the nature of the soil is called, is between pH5 (moderately acid) and pH7 (neutral) although in practice it will be found that they tolerate alkaline soils as long as plenty of organic material is present. If leafmould is used it is better to obtain it from other than an alkaline soil, for the pH of such material can be surprisingly high. The same applies to spent hops and old mushroom compost, both of which often contain lumps of chalk. Spent hops direct from the brewery, keeping that distinctive beery smell when delivered, are among the most useful of all materials. Use them for digging-in and mulching: there is no need to rot them down before use as they are completely harmless in their fresh state. With added fertiliser, hops make a good substitute for farmyard manure which is always in short supply.

Where the fuchsias are to follow spring bedding the area will not be available for autumn preparation in this way, consequently there will be less time to carry out the deep digging usually advocated. In this event it will be easier if the manure is spread on the surface of the cleared bed before digging in. The manure or other material being used should be at least partly rotted when using this method, for contact with fresh manure could be fatal to tender roots.

Planting out

For out of doors, choose the more vigorous growing cultivars for preference, as they usually out-perform any with a weak constitution in the tough conditions they are likely to encounter. Generally speaking, the larger the plant when it goes in, the sooner a good display is furnished. For this purpose there is no reason why the plants should not be brought on under glass before planting out. They can be either grown from cuttings or purchased and, providing they are well hardened off, can be put out as soon as danger from frost has passed. In the event of a late

A method of frost protection for young plants.

spring frost occurring, sheets of newspaper will go a long way towards protecting new growth. Lay the paper over the whole plant, secure it with stones and remove it next morning. The same planting instructions apply to the hardy fuchsias that are to remain where they are planted; here it is even more important to see that they have a good start in life with a soil that has been adequately prepared.

Planting takes place when the ground is ready, with the soil in a satisfactory condition to receive them. Delay planting when it is cold or wet. Should the opposite apply, it is in order to water the ground the night before setting the plants out. When the intention is to allow the fuchsias to remain as permanent subjects they must be planted with the crown well below soil level as an insurance against frost damage. The depth will vary from 3 to 9 in (7.5–23 cm) depending on the vigour of the cultivar. Fuchsias are what are generally termed 'gross feeders' – a polite way of saying that they are greedy plants! They will respond very quickly to heavily manured or fertilised ground. The danger lies in the fact that under these conditions too much leafy growth can be produced at the expense of flowers. Worse than this is the

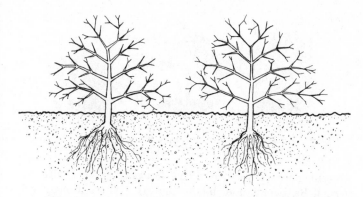

When planting, the crown must be well below ground level to avoid frost damage.

possibility that stems will not ripen properly nor sufficient new roots form to carry the plant through the winter. At the same time they will require a light sprinkling of a slow-release general fertiliser put on at planting and carefully raked in. Do not overdo this. The fertiliser will do its work over several weeks but should an added boost be felt necessary a foliar feed can be sprayed on the leaves once or twice during the growing season.

Mulching

A mulch of an organic material such as peat, leafmould (especially that made from rotted bracken) or garden compost, placed around the plants when the soil is moist, will help conserve moisture, improving the soil texture too when it is dug in later. Granulated sphagnum moss peat is favoured by ourselves for this purpose as it is so easy to obtain and certainly gives good results. It has little feeding value in it so it should be used in conjunction with the slow-release fertiliser mentioned above. Spread it on the soil only after it has been thoroughly moistened, for if it is used in a dry state rain can only permeate with the greatest difficulty. Ensure that the plants never dry out by

39

*An organic mulch around the base of the plant
helps conserve moisture.*

watering during dry weather. This does not apply very often in a normal British summer but in countries where drought conditions prevail it is more important. An overhead spray in the evening with a syringe or fine rose water can will be much appreciated by fuchsias after a hot day – a requirement that is inherited from their wild ancestors which receive an abundance of moisture in those countries where 'the rain it raineth every day and every night also'.

Decorative hedges

As a decorative hedge for summer display the fuchsia has few rivals, for there are not many shrubs that can boast of continuous flowering from early summer until the frosts. This form of hedge is a feature of many coastal towns but there is no reason why, if care is taken with the siting of the plants, they should not thrive just as well inland. As it is intended that this is to be a permanent planting, extra work on the preparation of the soil is required. Dig out a trench along the line the hedge is to take, placing the top spit to one side. Remove the second spit altogether and break the subsoil with a fork without turning it over. The trench is now almost filled with prepared garden compost or well rotted manure, trodden down and the top spit replaced. A sprinkling of steamed bonemeal is put on, raked in and the ground is ready for planting. Should the finished level of the trench be slightly below that of the surrounding soil then so

For a hedge, plant the fuchsias in the normal way, with the crown well below soil level, about 18 in (45 cm) apart.

much the better, for this space can be filled in with a further mulch of sieved garden compost during the growing season. Place the plants along the row remembering to keep the crown (i.e. the point at which roots and stem are joined) several inches below soil level for winter protection. Spacing depends on the vigour of the cultivar chosen; 18 in (45 cm) apart is the average.

Other uses for hardy fuchsias

Hardy fuchsias are well suited for filling up spaces in the shrub border, where they add colour when it is most needed, and over a long period. Bold planting is the most effective treatment using at least three plants in a group. Each group should be of the same cultivar to give a really bright show. The coloured foliage of the hardy *F. magellanica* 'Variegata' shows up particularly well when planted with say *Caryopteris* or *Ceratostigma*. Interplanted with winter flowering heaths, some of the hardier cultivars give a good display when their jewel-like colours are set off to perfection against the green foil of the heaths' summer foliage. We have 'Alice Hoffman', 'Margaret' and 'Tom Thumb' planted in such a manner. They get pruned back to ground level very early each spring as the heathers are coming into flower. The new shoots of the fuchsias come to no harm under the protection of the dense cover of the heaths' evergreen foliage.

41

After the initial riot of colour is over on the rock garden in summer, there is often little to be seen until the late autumn flowering alpines are out. During this lull in the late summer the little fuchsias come into their own. These tiny growers, unlike many subjects planted for summer colour, have a perfect right to be included in a collection of alpines, for the name alpine does not signify that a plant comes from the Alps but from a high place. This many of the wild fuchsias do, for some have been seen growing at altitudes of over 10,000 ft (3,700 m). A personal favourite in this situation is the lovely little *F.* 'Pumila'. Plant them in groups in the full sun and they will not disappoint you.

4
Greenhouse Cultivation

Owning a greenhouse, or in warm countries a shade or lath house, is a great asset in the successful cultivation of the fuchsia. Although by no means essential they give more control over the subject than is possible outside; for example where a greenhouse is used a start to the growing season can be made much earlier. Just how early will depend on whether heating is installed or not – a temperature of 13°C (55°F) should be the aim. An early start means that flowers are produced on a larger plant and over a longer period than can be expected from those grown solely in the open. Of almost equal importance to warmth for the growing plant is the way in which humidity can be controlled more easily. To sum up, the advantages of using a permanent structure for growing fuchsias is twofold. Firstly, for winter shelter, it provides a good start for the plants which will go into the garden later; secondly, it can house a collection of plants for the more serious grower on a more or less year-round basis. We say more or less because many do in fact stand their potted plants outside, and even more people bed them in the soil for a few weeks during the hottest part of the year when they prove a welcome addition to the garden display. To save time on watering the pots, especially those of the clay type, they can be plunged to their rim in the soil. When the watering is done it is an advantage to the fuchsias if an area around the pot gets watered too.

At the end of Chapter 2 it was explained how young plants purchased from a nursery are potted on into larger pots as soon as ready in order to keep them growing freely. Frequent overhead syringing keeps the foliage crisp whilst also discouraging attack from red spider mite. Overhead spraying may be stopped when the plants commence blooming.

Shading

To prevent the atmosphere in the house from becoming too dry, some form of shading must be employed as the days get hotter. For a greenhouse, roller blinds that are attached to the ridge can be let down on sunny days or pulled up when dull. These are best but many simply resort to shading painted on the outside of the glass. Ventilation should be attended to each day in order to maintain a buoyant atmosphere with a good circulation of air. Temperatures must not be allowed to rise too high: the plants will fare better under cool conditions. The great fluctuations of temperature experienced in small glass structures are a big drawback making efficient shading even more important here.

Training

While a plant is still young a decision has to be taken on the ultimate form of the mature specimen, for fuchsias can be trained in all manner of ways, the outcome depending largely on the natural form of the cultivar chosen, as well as the skill of the grower. Strong upright growers make the best standards; lax trailing forms are a 'natural' for hanging baskets but are also effectively utilised for pyramids or bush forms.

In order to get the best from any given plant the growing tips have to be pinched out to shape the growth. This summer pruning as it is sometimes called can be done with the fingernails when the growth is tender, but if it is left a little too long a small pair of secateurs will do the job. Make sure that they are sharp!

The training that is carried out in the first season sets the pattern for the whole of the life of the plant, and once spoiled the shape is often difficult to rectify, although if a mistake occurs one can usually turn a plant back into a bush shape. Many taking up the growing of fuchsias for the first time are a little dubious about pinching out nice growing tips or removing flower buds from immature plants. What must be remembered about growing this group of plants in pots is that it is an unnatural life for them, and therefore they are subject to methods that are not used for plants growing in the soil.

Bush

For a bush plant, the most popular form, it is usual to allow four sets of leaves to develop before pinching out the growing tip. When three sets have formed on the resulting laterals, pinch out the tips of the laterals. This will be sufficient for an average plant, but to produce a specimen of the type seen at flower shows impose a further stop after three more sets of leaves have grown. This will result in a superb well-branched plant. Many cultivars

Bush

will be found to branch naturally even without any pinching out, but these too will be better if stopped rather than left to their own devices.

Standard

A standard is really only a bush on a tall stem and has the advantage that flowers can be viewed easily even when the pot is stood on the ground. Planted out there is no fear that the blossoms will be damaged by soil splashing on them. To commence the training of a standard the single stem must be allowed to grow unstopped until the required height is reached. The young stems which are known as whips can either be purchased the previous season or be grown from cuttings. In both cases they will need to be kept growing during the winter period to ensure a thick stem to carry the head of flowers the following season. A stout trunk will be produced by a strong growing cultivar, whereas one with

Standard

46

a trailing habit will only be coaxed up the support with some difficulty. During the winter the young plants do not require a great amount of heat, just sufficient to keep the air above freezing. The more quickly a stem can be run up the better the chances are that it will be straight. Feeding with a liquid fertiliser containing more nitrogen than is normal for fuchsias will encourage suitable lush growth. This may be given at two-week intervals but only when the young plant is growing freely. The nitrogenous feed may be alternated with the normal weekly feeding programme (see p. 54) until the whip is stopped for the first time. When a proprietary brand is used keep to the manufacturer's recommended strength without trying to hurry things along. Stems are usually allowed to reach 36–40 in (90–100 cm) high before removing the growing tip. Pinch out at least twice more each time the laterals make three or four sets of leaves. A better head will develop from a stem that produces leaves in threes rather than the usual pairs and these plants can often be selected when still in the young stage. Side growths that develop on the main stem below the head must be removed as they appear, taking care to leave the foliage intact; this is not taken off until the training is complete with the flowers about to appear.

Standards are always staked securely throughout their life. Where several are being grown the individual canes can be tied to a cross wire to prevent accidental damage while growth is still very soft.

Basket

Hanging baskets, either circular or semicircular, are a fine way of growing fuchsias, and the pendant growth of many of the best cultivars lends itself to this type of feature. Here, the cascading flowers can trail with no fear of becoming damaged as they could be if planted in the soil. A well-filled round basket planted with say three plants of the current season, or a good size specimen in a half basket, will make a colourful display in the greenhouse, patio or porch. Keep to one cultivar in each container, for when mixed the varying rate of growth of each plant can lead to a lop-sided effect. The growing season needs to be fairly long if the baskets are needed for display over the greater part of the summer. This makes the greenhouse essential in the early stages although it is not needed when well-grown plants are purchased ready for filling the basket. For the really pendant cultivars the

Basket

small plants are started in pots and allowed to produce four sets of leaves before stopping. Only two of the resulting shoots are retained. These are encouraged to grow without further stopping so that when put into the basket they reach the rim before break-ing. Pinching-out is done as each shoot reaches the three leaf stage. Timing the flowers so that they open on a certain date can be done by remembering that it will take about six weeks from the time of the last stop. If flower buds are removed up to this time the final display will be the better for it.

Fuchsias in baskets require a great deal of water in a dry spell. Under these conditions every evening will not be too often to take the basket down. Half immerse it in water until saturated, allowing it to drain before replacing. While the basket is down go over the plants to check for insect pests, remove spent flowers and dead foliage.

Fan

A fan-trained fuchsia can, with skill, be induced to cover a wall or fence in a relatively short time if a strong grower is selected. Start the training with a young plant, allowing it to grow three sets of leaves before pinching out the tip. Using a light framework for support, tie in the resultant breaks carefully before stopping the growth again when a further three sets of leaves have developed. Always choose the strongest shoot that grows at each break, tying it in to form the rays of a fan. Remove unwanted growth altogether and keep the laterals that will bear the flowers pinched well back until the shape is well formed.

Fan

Climber

Another method of training some fuchsias is to treat them as climbers. They are not climbers in the true sense of the word so will need to be pinched back and tied in carefully until they cover the roof supports with their mass of pendulous flowers. Looking up into the blooms from below one gets a completely different impression of their shape and colouration, which makes this way of growing so worth while where the right conditions for winter protection are possible. A vigorous growing young plant is allowed to grow away with a single leader by removing side growths as they appear. Once the leader has grown to a reasonable height, two lateral shoots are left to develop and are tied in with it. (The height at which the climber is allowed to keep these side growths depends on the position in which it is planted; sometimes they will be left just above the ground level but more often from above the staging.) Pruning consists of spurring back all side growths to one or two buds in winter and pinching out the tips of new shoots twice to ensure plenty of flowering wood.

Pyramid

The pyramid shape is not for the beginner, but with experience it will make a fine way of growing a specimen plant that will, with care, last for many seasons. Some pyramids we have seen are really a bush shape with a standard growing on the same root. Very briefly (for each has his own method of getting such a

Pyramid

Column

result) the training is as follows. An unstopped shoot is tied loosely to a strong stake and is allowed to run up to 12 in (30 cm), then stopped. All the laterals are pinched out as soon as they have formed two sets of leaves, with the exception of one of the topmost shoots, the strongest, which is tied in to the stake to make a new leader. This in turn is stopped when the required height has been reached with all of its laterals pinched back as they each form two sets of leaves. An experienced grower will, by the time the flowering starts, have a mass of blooms from the laterals spaced nicely around the well-supported plant which tapers from the base to the tip. A 'cascade' or trailing cultivar is often used with spectacular results although it will require much work and will need two complete seasons with a dormant period in between before the effect is achieved.

Column

The column shape is another way of growing fuchsias in which the expert pits his skill against the plant's natural reluctance to grow in a narrow column, for left to themselves most plants would grow into a loose bush, whereas others would trail about over the ground. A column will need a strong grower, a strong stake and a strong will, for this is another form that takes a minimum of two seasons' growth to obtain. There is more than one way of obtaining the desired form but the easiest is to tie an unstopped plant to the stake, pinching back the laterals to a single pair of leaves as they are formed. The secret is to be able to time the flowering so that all the flowers open at the same time. The only way to ensure this is to see that each lateral is stopped on the same occasion, allowing a minimum of six weeks to flowering time.

Staking

Many of the half-hardy summer bedding fuchsias, as well as those used for greenhouse decoration, will be better if supported. All that is required is a light cane with a single loop of wool right round the plant. Try to keep any canes as unobtrusive as possible, otherwise the decorative effect of the plant will be spoiled.

Standards, whether indoors or out, will always need a stake, in this case extending the height of the stem including the head. The head, once developed, should also receive some additional support from stiff wires extending from the top of the stake down and outwards rather in the fashion of the ribs of an umbrella, although not as numerous. If the end of the wire is bent into a tight hook each main lateral can be lifted over it carefully before the opening flowers develop much weight. This considerably lessens the risk of shedding a branch. For those plants that are destined for hanging baskets, the light cane support is removed when the fuchsia has been planted in the basket, and the stems can then trail over in a natural manner.

A single cane is needed for pyramids, but be prepared to give additional support with wires to the lower or central parts of the plants if necessary. The taller the fuchsia is allowed to go the more support is likely to be needed.

When fuchsias are being trained in a fan shape, a light framework is employed when the young plant is still in a pot prior to planting out. Wires stretched between suitable nails fixed to the fence or wall can cover the area the mature shrub is likely to reach. These are fixed in position before the plant is set out. The temporary framework used with the pot-grown plant is removed at planting time when the partly trained branches are tied in lightly with soft wool along the wire supports.

How to stake a standard, using additional wire support for the head.

Some of the cultivars that are grown inside will be better for supporting. When starting off the supports should be of the lightest cane, getting more substantial as the plant matures. Insert the sharpened stake with great care to avoid damaging fleshy roots. Several materials are suitable for tying, e.g. wool or raffia. We use ready-made covered wire ties which are very quick in use, only needing a single twist to secure or remove. Be careful not to restrict the flow of the sap by tying too tightly, for tiny stems can swell considerably during the course of a full season.

Feeding

Pot-grown fuchsias are among the few plants that really need feeding throughout their growing season. In addition to the solid fertiliser contained in the compost, a liquid feed will ensure a continuance of satisfactory growth with flowers of better colour and more substance. Where plants are growing in soilless composts, extra feeding is even more important owing to their initial lower nutrient content. Although solid material can be used to give that added boost, more control is made available by using liquid feeding which is immediately taken up by the plant. An application once a week will be in order when the plants are growing freely except where repotting has just been done. Use a preparation with a high potash content (K_2O) to ensure plentiful flowers carried on solid stems. As with all feeding of plants a little now and then is better than a heavy dose at infrequent intervals. Should the plant be unable to take up the proffered nutrient for some reason or other, the leaves take on a yellowish hue with distinct green veining. When this happens, discontinue application until foliage returns to normal. There are some cultivars in which a slight yellowing of the foliage is perfectly normal; the very beautiful 'Morning Light' is one of these. Another occasion when foliage turns the wrong colour, in this case purplish, is when plants are taken from a warm greenhouse into colder outdoor conditions. Except in extreme cases plants make a good recovery to flower normally during the season.

Greenhouse displays

Nearly all fuchsias seen inside are either in pots or hanging in baskets, but they need not be confined to this way of growing.

54

Planting directly in a border that has been well prepared is one of the easiest methods of cultivation and certainly the finest way of displaying them in a natural manner. Imagination plays a big part in the ultimate success of a fuchsia border, for the grouping of the colours so that they harmonise is most important. To commence, the plants are grown normally in pots until well established and are trained for bush shape and so on as required. Tall growers, perhaps with a standard or two, are planted in the centre of the bed first to give height. Bush forms are kept near the front, together with trailers which should be at the edge near the path. It may be that the border is not very wide, in which case the taller growers will have to be alternated with the low or more compact forms. Where there is a wall to the rear a fan-trained specimen will provide a good backdrop.

Should any other plants be put in with the fuchsias? This a personal decision. Ferns of many species, *Coleus, Impatiens,* etc. are all natural companions, although we feel that the enthusiast will want to grow as many fuchsias as he can from the wide range available including the fascinating species. A border planted with fuchsias in this way need not be regarded as a temporary home, for provided the soil is in good heart when they go in the fuchsias will last and thrive for many seasons. The occasional ailing specimen can be taken out to be replaced with something new that has caught the eye. Do not crowd the plants when first setting out, for they do not care for too much competition at the roots, nor do the flowers display as well when branches intertwine. Most fuchsias are not really hot house plants but the best flowers are seen in cooler conditions. This is a help in winter for they do not need much heat. Provided that the temperature does not drop below 5°C (40°F) they should come through unharmed. Some of the species are better off at slightly higher temperatures than these, making artificial heating a 'must'. Water sparingly during the cold months so that the plants become semi-dormant. When the warmer days start in spring, pruning can be done according to needs, a dressing of a complete fertiliser given and a mulch of fresh soil or well-rotted manure spread over the bed.

In the cold greenhouse (or shade house in a warm climate) fuchsias are best treated in the same way as the more tender sorts used outdoors; that is to say they must be allowed to become dormant after the main flowering is over and stored in a frost-free situation until starting up again in the spring. (For more details see p. 61.) Pot plants display better if grown on staging rather than on the floor. Not only is management easier at this height but the flowers are nearer eye level and can be viewed more easily. Do not crowd the pots on the staging, for the individual plants will grow better with less likelihood of pests being overlooked when they are spaced out. Give the pots a half turn every few days to get a nicely balanced plant, for otherwise they tend to grow towards the light on one side.

Hanging baskets can be purchased, made from galvanised wire, plastic or wood. Our own favourites are the teak baskets normally used for the culture of orchids, which display fuchsias in a most natural manner. Except for some of the plastic types a lining of green moss is placed first to stop the compost from washing through. Where this is difficult to come by, green polythene has been used as a substitute.

No greenhouse? This need not deter anyone from growing fuchsias in pots for use on the patio or in window boxes. Treatment is basically the same as when they are grown in a cold greenhouse. Young plants are purchased in the spring, potted-on as required using a cold frame or even a window-sill for the early stages. When the summer is over they can be discarded or stored in a frost-free place until the following spring. Growth is restarted by bringing them out, watering, pruning and repotting (see p. 61).

House plants

Many of the large flowered modern cultivars of fuchsia that grace our greenhouse do not take kindly to cultivation in the home as a house plant. They invariably show their displeasure first of all by dropping all their flowers as soon as they are brought indoors, then soon afterwards shedding their foliage. Yet the Victorian housewives used the fuchsia with great success. In spite of flickering gas lights, the greatest killer of all house plants, many thousands are said to have been purchased for this purpose. It is the dry atmosphere present in today's homes that is their dislike, for the murky conditions present in the previous era suited the fuchsias more than the light, bright atmosphere we all enjoy today. The type of plants they used were of the smaller-flowered, almost hardy kinds that can still be purchased. Try 'Princess Dollar', 'Port Arthur' or 'Gloire de Marche'. If these are selected, placed on a gravel tray in light conditions but not too sunny, there is no reason why they cannot be used as flowering house plants. They must never be allowed to dry out when in active growth but as the days grow shorter less water may be given. Dormancy is finally brought about by withholding water almost altogether. Pots may be stood outside in sunny weather to ripen the wood before they are placed in a cupboard, shed or cellar until the spring. Repotting is not as important for house plant fuchsias as for those in the greenhouse, for as long as some of the old compost is replaced with fresh each spring the plants should thrive, but they must be pruned back well each year. Like many other house plants, fuchsias enjoy being stood outside in a gentle shower, but do not wait for rain to cleanse the foliage. This should be done regularly with a piece of cotton wool soaked in water. Regular feeding is important to maintain active growth and a watch should be kept for pests of which greenfly is usually the most troublesome.

5
Preparing for Dormancy

In the autumn, after a frost has burned the foliage, it will be time to prepare the outdoor fuchsias for their dormant or resting period. Except in the very mildest climate some form of protection will be advisable even for the hardy cultivars. On the rockery or in the shrub border it is normally enough to draw some of the surrounding soil towards the centre of the plant so that the crown is well covered. A layer of dry peat 6 in (15 cm) deep will prove a good insulation against most frosts; some flat stones can be laid on this leaving the crown clear. These stones will hold the material in place until the spring when they can be removed, while the peat which remains will act as a mulch. At the same time the stems are pruned back to living wood and the new shoots will grow away strongly even if the plant has been cut by frost almost to ground level.

Where established hedges are concerned a little more attention is needed. Here, as in the case of single plants, draw soil over the crowns; peat or weathered ash may be used instead. At the same time, weave dry bracken or straw in and around the lower stems to protect them from the worst of the weather. In really cold gardens plants may also require a sheet of polythene to be secured around the outside in a tent-like fashion. Plants trained against a wall are usually much safer from the effects of harsh weather than similar plants in the open, although even here it is good sense to provide some cover for the lower stems down to soil level. This insulation remains in position until the spring when the bracken or straw is removed carefully to avoid damaging the emerging shoots. In instances where plants have been found to have been killed back, delay the pruning until the extent of the damage is clearly seen. Where a hedge has come through the dormant time well, most of the framework of branches will be intact. The time to prune will be when new shoots are seen breaking into growth. Take off all weak, thin or badly placed stems of the previous season and reduce any dead branches back to living wood.

A method of winter protection using polythene.

Summer bedders

A different treatment is accorded to those fuchsias that have been grown as summer bedding. These are unable to remain in their positions, for other plants will occupy the space they vacate ready for the spring display. As with the hardy cultivars, wait until shorter days terminate growth for the season before lifting the plants which need a frost-free place for the winter. This can be a greenhouse, cold-frame, shed or cellar – some enthusiasts have even been known to accommodate them in a spare bedroom! After lifting, place the plants in an airy spot to allow the soil surrounding the root ball to become partially dry. Before plunging in leaves, bracken, straw or peat the plants should be tidied up by reducing the size of the root ball, and trimming of withered shoots or broken growths. Do not allow the roots to become totally dry at any time during the dormancy. Check on their condition now and then preferably during a mild spell. Any dry, mildew-affected leaves should be taken off when the plants are being looked at and the stems sprayed lightly with water to keep them fresh. They should be allowed to dry off again before replacing their protective covering.

Where no building is available for winter storage the dormant plants can often be accommodated in a sheltered spot outside. Choose an out-of-the-way place for this, perhaps an empty border sheltered by a wall (this will be perfect, for a wall makes the finest windbreak of all). The fuchsias are plunged quite thickly in the soil and after plants are tidied by reducing the length of the old flowering stems by about a third the process of insulation can begin. Once again use dry bracken leaves or straw to cover the roots, extending the material upwards through the branches until the plants are completely buried. Some fuchsia growers use a low temporary structure with chicken wire to hold the chosen insulating material. Others simply bury the plants in a trench dug in the soil which is filled with leaves, or if the ground is light the soil is used to fill the trench in. Should you choose the latter method do not forget where you buried them when spring comes around! When the worst of the frosts are past is the time to uncover your hibernating stock.

Pruning must now be done, firstly to repair any damage the winter has inflicted, but also to make sure that the plant will be sturdy with plenty of vigour. Dead wood is cut back to living tissue, weakly-looking growths are also removed. The laterals are pruned to within two or three leaf nodes of the previous season's growth from the main stems on a typical bush shape, although this does vary according to shape and cultivar. As soon as the prepared site is ready again set them out as before. When a late frost is forecast the tender new shoots can receive the protection of a sheet of newspaper tied lightly in position overnight.

Plants in pots

Pot-grown, the fuchsias are not as a rule very long-lived plants —
any that have passed their third birthday are often past their
best. However, a plant in good heart need not be disposed of at
the end of the season. Pot-grown specimens that have been used
as plants for patio or garden decoration, as summer bedders or in
the greenhouse are overwintered inside in a similar manner to
that set out above. They can be kept without any bother where
heat is installed, but even in a cold house protection is easily
effected.

To prepare for dormancy the pots are placed along the path-
way of the greenhouse, but watering is gradually withheld until
the plants are fairly dry with most of the foliage having fallen.
Do not hurry this process or allow the pots to become dust dry at
any time. Plunge the pots to their rims under the staging if the
position is suitable, with a thick layer of peat or leaves over the
crowns. In a cold house additional covering will be required to
make sure that frost does not reach the roots. Pots need not be
kept in the light so a cellar or shed will suit just as well. Check on
their condition now and again and give a light spray to freshen
them up.

Starting up in spring

When cuttings are required for fresh stock, plants are started
into growth fairly early in the new year but if there is no urgency
it may be left until late spring.

When ready to start, give the pots a thorough soak. Do not
attempt the pruning yet but clean the plants by removing all old
foliage. One watering should be sufficient to induce the dormant
buds to swell, while a gentle spray with tepid water will also help.
Only after the buds have started to grow can the pruning and repotting be done. Tackle the pruning first. As all flowers are
carried on the current year's growth only, there is little need to

Prune back lateral growths to within two or three buds of the main stem.

keep any more of the old wood than is required to maintain the framework of the plant once the shape has been determined. In practice, most of the shoots produced the previous season are removed by spurring back lateral growths to within two or three buds of the main stems, making the cut to a sprouting bud. At this time it is a good plan to clean old bark from the stems of standards by rubbing gently with a soft nylon brush that has been moistened.

Potting-back is the next job to be tackled. To do this shake out, or if preferred carefully wash away, as much of the old compost as possible before potting back using a suitable compost (see p. 28) in a smaller size pot. Water the plant to re-establish it and give shade if the sunshine is very bright until growth starts. The growing cycle of repotting, feeding and stopping can now recommence.

The traditional time for taking cuttings is after growth has started.

6
Raising New Stock

In previous chapters we have talked only of purchasing plants from a nurseryman. Once a stock has been obtained in this way there is no reason why additional plants should not be raised at home using propagating material from one's own plants or pieces donated by friends. Fortunately for us fuchsias are among the gardening world's more easily increased subjects. Vegetative methods of increasing the stock are essential if the true character of any cultivar or clone is to be retained. Cuttings, usually in a half-ripe state, are universally employed for this, as grafting is an art seldom, if ever, employed nowadays. The keen amateur may care to try his hand at grafting as a novelty, although it has very limited practical use for fuchsias.

The third way to increase plants is from seed. It is interesting to experiment in order to see just what will materialise, and most new sorts come about in this way. These are of course the result of careful breeding, many hundreds being discarded before a novelty is considered fit for marketing.

Cuttings

Cuttings will strike readily at any time during the active growing season but the best results are obtained before the wood matures. Half-ripe cuttings taken before the summer sun gets too hot will be easier to handle, root quicker and, if taken early enough, will produce a good show of flowers in the first season.

In order to produce plants of quality it is essential to select only first class stock. Choose sturdy, straight stems with short spaces between the nodes or leaf joints. Ignore thin shoots or those where the foliage is spaced widely apart, although some cultivars do not grow in a way that is ideal for taking cuttings.

Dormant plants which have been potted back, watered and then pruned make fairly rapid growth in early spring. New shoots appearing after the old twigs are spurred back are allowed to grow until they bear some four pairs of leaves together with a plump tip. Remove the selected cutting with a sharp razor blade, leaving two pairs of leaves on the plant from which further shoots will spring. Fuchsias will root from cuttings that are cut between the nodes although most people prefer to cut just below the leaf joint and remove the lower pair of leaves. After removal, these cuttings are inserted into a compost that retains moisture, is sharply drained to remove excess water and is well aerated. J. I. seed with a little extra sand, or a mixture of medium grade sphagnum moss peat and clean sharp river sand in equal proportions, will give consistently good results as a substrate or rooting medium. There are many other suitable materials such as moist peat, sand, sandy compost, vermiculite, pumice or even water.

Where only a small quantity of plants is needed, sufficient cuttings can be placed around the edge of a pot; larger numbers are better planted in trays. Label immediately with the name of the cultivar for the memory is remarkably fickle. Where a propagating bench complete with intermittent mist is available use it, for fuchsias respond very well to these conditions. Failing this, place pots or boxes of cuttings in a warm part of the greenhouse or frame, keeping the foliage turgid with a light overhead spray when needed. Bottom heat will also be beneficial and rooting will take place remarkably quickly under conditions that are ideal. We have had good results when a polythene bag has been placed over the rim of the pot after the cuttings have been put in. Only one watering is normally enough when this is done, for moisture given off by the foliage is trapped, running back down the inside of the bag into the pot. Also of value when only a few plants are needed and no heating is available are the clear plastic covers that are made to fit both pots and trays; these create just the sort of micro-climate that fuchsias enjoy. When light green tips appear, indicating that the cuttings are rooting, more air must be admitted. It is best to pot on as soon as possible in order that the little plants many not receive a check by remaining too long in a medium that lacks nutrient. J. I. 2 potting compost is our choice for the growing-on period using small pots for the initial move.

Another type of cutting, from which many specimen plants are

A half-ripe cutting prepared for insertion.

produced for display the following season, is started from short-jointed, half-ripened shoots taken off the plant for rooting during the summer. Where no greenhouse is available this method will prove a good alternative to striking plants in the spring. Now they can be rooted with the sun's warmth, kept in a sunny window and overwintered before potting on or planting out the following late spring. On many plants it is not easy to find the correct type of shoots to use, as all are flowering profusely at this season; so some of the branches should be cut back four weeks before taking cuttings. The cuttings are prepared in a similar way to that described for rooting in the spring (p. 61). After insertion they are watered, then placed in a partly shaded spot in the greenhouse, frame or even outdoors until rooted. If taken early in the summer they can be potted on as soon as they have rooted sufficiently, using a free-draining compost. This can be standard J. I. 2 or a home-made mixture with a small quantity of a slow-release fertiliser added. The first potting in small pots will carry the plants through the winter without further feeding. They should be placed in a light airy place in the greenhouse or by a window. If temperatures are kept slightly above freezing growth will stagnate during the dull days of winter, so keep the compost rather dry but do not allow it to dry out completely. Growth will become more active as the temperatures rise in the spring; at this time a sharp watch must be kept for insects.

The normal potting-on procedure carries on from this point. Where whips are being grown for training as standards do not remove the growing tip but all others can be stopped (see p. 45).

Grafting

Grafting can be employed where a good weeping head of a desired cultivar is wanted on a stout stem. Because of their form many of the best of the cascade type of cultivar do not have the

A method of grafting fuchsias.

ability to make a straight stem even with careful training. It is sometimes possible to employ a vigorous grower to furnish the trunk (stock) while the weaker-growing more desirable kind (scion) is grafted in at the required height to form the head. The easiest and most suitable method of grafting fuchsias is to inarch to two plants. This can often be observed in the wild where two branches of a tree have crossed and a natural union takes place as they grow. In the case of the fuchsia, two plants still in their pots are placed adjacently and a sliver of bark is removed from near the top of the standard at the point where the join is to take place. A corresponding piece of bark is cut away from a strong ripe shoot of the plant that is to form the head. The two cut surfaces are brought together quickly and bound with a strip of polythene. Tie this in place but remember to check for tightness as growth commences. When a complete union is judged to have taken place the scion is cut away from the parent. All other growth is now removed from the stock, both below and above the join, so that all the energy is passed entirely to the recipient. The growing shoot must be supported throughout its life if the two halves of the plant are not to part company, for although they are joined with living tissue there is a risk of a break owing to the brittle growth. Any buds that develop below the union must be rubbed out for they tend to take over the energy of the plant.

Seed

The third way of raising plants is from seed. Although this is the way most new cultivars of fuchsias are raised it does not mean that every seedling that flowers is a winner; in fact more often than not the opposite is true. Deliberate cross-pollination is slightly different, for here the hybridist has a definite objective in mind. It may be a new colour, or even a combination of colours, but it is more likely to be a plant of better constitution or habit of growth. Even so, many hundreds of seedlings are raised each year only to be discarded as their faults appear. If all this has not put the reader off sowing seeds we will proceed to the method commonly employed.

The seeds are contained in a berry or fleshy capsule which, incidentally, is perfectly edible although rather insipid to the taste. We came across a recipe in an old book for a tart made from fuchsia berries but from the amount of lemon juice required we suspect that this would be the dominant flavour. Most writers advocate squashing the purple or green ripe berries in order to extract the seeds; we find it better to dissect them one at a time using a razor blade. The seeds are scraped out onto a sheet of blotting paper which absorbs most of the water contained with them. Whenever possible, it is best to sow them immediately for then germination is rapid. They are sown in a light, fine, sterilised compost with a minimum covering of silver sand and carefully watered. The pots are shaded with brown paper then placed in a warm place for germination to take place. Check on development now and then, removing the shading as the tiny seed leaves appear. Sown thinly, they can remain in this container in a frost-free place until the following spring when potting-off into individual pots is done. Some of the best sorts seem to come from the weaker-looking seedlings so do not discard these until all have flowered. When it is not convenient to sow at once leave the seeds on blotting paper in a sunny place until dry. They are then packeted (together with a record of the cross if it has been deliberate) to be sown the following spring. It is always doubtful whether fuchsia seed will germinate but the best results always come from earlier sowings. Should something appear that seems to be really distinct from any other fuchsias known to the raiser, it is best to check with a specialist before naming. He will have a mental picture of every fuchsia he knows and will be able to advise on the worth of your new plant. When it proves to be distinct from others in cultivation it can receive a name, after propagating. This must be done vegetatively to ensure that the offspring are all identical to the original, as there is little likelihood of their reverting as has sometimes happened when a new plant is raised from a sporting bud. You can call your offspring anything you like providing the name complies with the International Code of Nomenclature for Cultivated Plants and the requirements of the Registration Authority (The American Fuchsia Society). Some of the finest cultivars of fuchsias have been raised by amateurs in the past, so in spite of the rather pessimistic start to this section a pot or two sown to see what comes up may well reward you for your time and patience with something really worthwhile.

7
Pests and Diseases

Pests

The saying 'the best form of defence is attack' might well origin-
ally have been coined by a gardener when describing how to deal
with glasshouse pests! In the case of the fuchsia this is
especially so, for once an infestation is allowed to take hold, although it may be possible to save the plants the damage already
caused may well spoil their decorative effect for the rest of the
season. Fuchsias are, however, comparatively free from such
things, particularly the hardy sorts.

Much good will be done when attention is paid conscientiously
to the normal cultural requirements of the plant. This means
that it is kept growing by repotting, maintaining a moist humid
atmosphere and spraying the foliage with water in the early
stages of growth. Shade from the hot sun should be provided
when needed. In hot dry conditions it is essential that the path-
ways and staging are kept well damped down, with attention
paid to ventilation so as to keep a buoyant circulation of air. Dry
air conditions favour the rapid increase of *red spider mite*, a
familiar glasshouse pest. Adults over-winter in crevices in the
glasshouse structure, staging and brickwork; bamboo canes,
straw or other litter also provide shelter. First steps should
therefore be towards cleanliness: the walls should be white-
washed or treated with a sterilant such as Jeyes Fluid during the
time the house is empty, and fumigation should be done at the

same time. The minute eggs hatch under a protective fine web made by the adult female. Newly hatched, the young feed by sucking the sap from the foliage of the fuchsia. Before long, mottled or even dead areas of tissue appear and leaves drop prematurely as a result of the interference with their normal function. Left unchecked the plants will become almost completely defoliated, and will sometimes die. A small hand sprayer is one of the best weapons for use in pest control. Filled with water that has had a drop or two of a wetting agent (i.e. soft detergent) added, it is directed towards the underside of the leaves to give them a thorough misting at frequent intervals. This is only partly preventative and is unlikely to lead to complete freedom from attack. When an infestation does occur fumigation or spraying with insecticide will have to be resorted to.

Red spider mites.

Fumigating a greenhouse is relatively easy these days if smoke cones are used. Read the instructions first. Remove any plants that are known to be prone to damage, close the house, place the cones in position, light those at the far end of the house first and retire immediately. If you are using several and one fails to ignite do not be tempted to re-enter to relight it as this could prove very uncomfortable, to say the least. The operation is best carried out overnight to avoid temperatures rising too high as would happen in a closed house on a hot day. In the morning, ventilate completely before going inside for any length of time. One of the problems of complete control of this pest is the ability of the mites to form an immune strain which shows resistance to the various chemicals used to combat it. Therefore, fumigation is not in itself sufficient to guarantee total kill; in view of this two or more materials should be used in rotation. The old-fashioned method of spraying with a soft soap solution is very effective against this pest. Soft soap is not stocked by sundriesmen as much now as formerly, in spite of its value in the garden.

Both this and the next insect pest can be partially controlled by the introduction into the greenhouse of special insect predators, but as these need a constant supply of pests to prey on they can hardly be regarded as a preventative measure. Fairly high temperatures are also needed before they do their stuff, so although in theory they sound the perfect way to a pest-free glasshouse to the best of our knowledge they are not entirely successful in practice.

Glasshouse white fly, young (right) and adult (left).

Glasshouse white fly or *ghost fly* as it is sometimes called has always been one of the worst pests to occur on fuchsias, although it infests many other species. Although it sometimes attacks plants growing outdoors in hot dry places which are adjacent to the greenhouse, it is most likely to cause trouble indoors. The green immature young hatch from eggs which are laid in clusters on the lower leaf surface. They crawl about for a short while before settling down to their scale-like stage. The perfect insects emerge from these scales appearing as tiny white moth-like creatures as they flit from plant to plant before settling. They are particularly noticeable when the plants are disturbed. The young feed on the sap, excreting considerable amounts of honeydew in the process. The sticky covering on the foliage breeds *sooty moulds* which although non-parasitic in themselves lead to unsightly fouling of both foliage and flowers. This also upsets the plants' normal respiratory system and results in premature leaf fall. With the *white fly* breeding takes place almost continuously throughout the year whenever temperatures are high enough, with several stages in the life cycle usually present under a leaf once the pest has gained a hold. Control of the adults is relatively easy, but the scale-like young often escape because they stay under the leaves where it is difficult to spray them. If they escape unharmed they will hatch out to continue breeding so that spraying at intervals is essential.

Modern insecticides, fungicides and acaricides (chemicals used for killing mites) can usually be purchased in handy aerosols which make the task of controlling attacks relatively easy. To save on costs small hand pressure sprayers can be used instead and filled with the dilute chemical as recommended by the manufacturer. Always treat these materials with the respect they deserve, adhering strictly to the instructions given on the container. Under glass it is not advisable to spray in hot sun or damage will result, so in warm weather wait until evening before spraying.

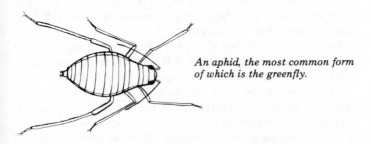

An aphid, the most common form of which is the greenfly.

Aphids are plant lice, several different species of which occur on young tender shoots both indoors and out. Colonies of these easily identified pests increase very rapidly if left unchecked but fortunately control is easy if regular attention is paid to the plants with a small hand sprayer filled with a suitable insecticide. Honeydew produced by these insects should be sponged from the foliage with a piece of moist cotton wool.

The waxy coating on the body of the *mealy bug* makes wetting by a pesticide rather difficult so that a bad attack, although rare, is most unwelcome. The adult females are wingless, but unlike the young which lead a sedentary existence they can move about. A dry atmosphere suits this pest and attacks often follow where the fuchsias are allowed to dry out frequently. Maintaining humidity will act as a splendid deterrent.

Ants can be blamed for the spread of mealy bugs both inside and out for they are fond of the honeydew which these pests secrete. The presence of this sticky substance on the foliage, together with its attendant growth of sooty mould, is often the first indication of an attack. An aerosol as suggested for aphids is the remedy. Ants, although not a pest in the usual sense of the word, cause trouble in two ways. Firstly, they will take a pot in which to carry out nest-building activities which causes disruption to the normal growth of the roots. Secondly, as has just been mentioned, they like honeydew, that sticky substance so liberally secreted by aphids, white fly and mealy bugs. Ants will move these pests around to fresh pastures in order to maintain a regular supply. Insecticide in a powder form dusted in and around pots or plants where the ants are seen will either kill them or discourage them from nesting.

Cyclamen mites do not often attack fuchsias but when they do it is invariably a plant that has suffered from too dry an atmosphere. These conditions are unhappily all too frequent in tiny glasshouses that are left unattended for many hours each day with the result that ventilation is not correctly carried out. Plants become stunted as a result of the presence of the mites in the roots and the foliage is mottled with rusty patches here and there. To clear up trouble remove the plant from the pot, shake off as much soil as possible and finally soak the roots in a mild insecticide for a few minutes. The plant can now be repotted in fresh compost and shaded for a day or two with frequent syringing of the foliage.

The *capsid bug* is a bright green insect that resembles a large slender aphid and which causes damage on fuchsias growing outside, although on occasion it will visit plants growing in greenhouses too. It has two distinct stages in its life cycle. The adult females lay their eggs on certain woody plants in the autumn; these hatch in the spring, soon becoming very active at feeding on the sap of the soft young shoots of the host plant. When partly grown they migrate by crawling to new plants — this is where the fuchsia is likely to be involved. Damage is caused by the bug injecting a toxic substance into the leaf on which it is feeding. To the capsid bug this saliva is only an aid to digestion but the plant cells react strongly to it by curling their leaves; the stems twist and curl with the flower buds often too distorted to open correctly. The normal method of control is to spray with a tar oil winter wash. This is fine on fruit trees and other hosts but of little use to fuchsia growers as the bugs are not present on fuchsias in winter. It is in the crawling stage that we have to counter them. Frequent spraying in early summer using the suggested insecticide (see pp. 76-7) should keep them in check.

A capsid bug.

PEST CONTROL CHART

		Azobenzine	BHC	Captan	Carbaryl
Aphids	Insects visible		S		
Ants	Insects visible		D		
Black Root Rot	Sudden wilting			W	
Capsid Bug	Insects visible		S		
Cyclamen Mite	Plant stunted		F*		
Fuchsia Rust	Visible on foliage				
Grey Mould	Foliage falls			S	
Mealy Bug	Visible under curled foliage		S		
Red Spider Mite	Foliage dries then falls	F			
Thrips	Foliage 'peppered'		S		
White Fly	Insects visible		D		
Vine Weevil	Unhealthy growth		D		D, W

Key: S=Spray D=Dust W=With water after attack
F=Fumigate F*=Fumigate after attack
F+=Fumigate at low overnight temperature

Clordane	Derris	Malathion	Maneb	Nicotine	Petroleum Oil	Tecnazine	Thiram	Zineb
	S, D	S, D		F, S	S			
S, W								
								S
		S		F, S				
		D						
			S				S	S
						F +	S	
		S, D			S			
	S			F	S			
	S			S, F	S			
				F				
		W						

77

An attack by *thrips* is another likely result of growing plants in adverse conditions. Bright light and dry air encourage these tiny black insects but it is the nymphs, as the young are called, that do the most damage. They hatch from minute eggs laid on the under leaf surfaces, feeding in colonies between the ribs of the leaf which becomes discoloured from their continual sucking of the sap. In a bad attack the whole of the under leaf surfaces are covered with a sticky black secretion which will ruin the plant if left unchecked. Control is by spraying.

When in the larval stage the *vine weevil* will feed on the roots of pot-grown plants making the leaves turn yellow and wilt in hot weather. It is not easy to control without removing all the soil from the root ball; the white grubs with brown heads will be seen when it is shaken off. The roots of the plant are soaked for a few moments in a mild solution of suitable insecticide before re-potting in fresh compost. Adult vine weevil feed at night eating out small pieces of foliage but in general are not as troublesome on fuchsias as on other plants such as ferns, *Primula* or saxifrage.

Caterpillars of various species of moth can sometimes be found chewing foliage. Pick these off as soon as seen.

Bees of different species can damage flowers and also by fertilising them whilst in search of nectar cause the flowers to fall immediately they mature. *Wasps* often eat large chunks of the flower. The only remedy is to provide ventilators and a door with netting of sufficiently small mesh to prevent their entry. *Leaf cutter bees* will on occasion trim neat pieces from leaves to use in nest-building. This is unfortunate if the specimen is destined for a show but otherwise best ignored.

From the pest control chart it will be seen that two methods (spraying and fumigating) will control most of the insects likely to be encountered in growing fuchsias. In practice either an aerosol or a small hand sprayer filled with a suitable insecticide (alone or in mixture) will be the most commonly used. Do not wait for an attack of aphids or white fly to occur before spraying but make up a small quantity every two weeks and go over the plants paying particular attention to the under leaf surfaces and growing tips.

Some troubles are not cured with the use of a sprayer but will need a fumigant or smoke cone which when lit sends off a dense cloud of insecticide filled smoke to permeate every part of the greenhouse structure. These can also be used as a preventative rather than cure.

Diseases

Fuchsia rust is sometimes recorded on fuchsias growing in greenhouses. Orange-yellow eruptions mostly occur on the under leaf surface, although in a bad attack the whole leaf will be covered. As the wild willow herb is frequently attacked, steps should be taken to ensure that it is eradicated from anywhere near the vicinity of the greenhouse. In the event of the disease affecting a fuchsia any foliage showing the symptoms must be removed from the plant before it falls, then burned to stop the spread of the fungus. As soon as the disease is suspected spray the plants with a fungicide at intervals until it is entirely cleared up.

Grey mould (Botrytis cinerea) occurs when a dank or humid, stuffy atmosphere persists. It can appear at any time of the year, young plants in winter being particularly prone to attack. All infected leaves should be picked off, for where they lie across a stem this will very often rot too. Maintaining a free flow of air usually clears up serious trouble; if not the house should be fumigated. Grey mould also affects plants growing outdoors when it rots flowers and foliage alike but fortunately this is almost always at the end of the season. When it happens try to allow the plants' foliage to dry off completely before bringing them inside. A dusting with a fungicide will help control the spread of the disease.

Yet another fungus disease to be on the look out for is *black root (Thielaviopsis basicola),* which is sometimes called *root-rot,*

79

for that is what it does. This soil- or water-borne fungus is normally encountered only in unsterilised compost, so we think it worth the effort to see that loam is treated before it is incorporated in potting materials. Roots turn black and rot as the fungus invades the cells which leads to a severe restriction in the growth of the plant. Foliage does not usually fall as might be expected but does wilt very easily as soon as the temperature rises. There are two methods of dealing with this trouble. The use of a systemic fungicide should be sufficient to control a mild attack, but when the attack is severe the plant must be removed from its pot, the compost removed, the dead roots cut away and the plant must be repotted in fresh sterilised compost. You should water with a mild fungicide two or three times every two weeks or so.

Not all problems are caused by pests and diseases. Physiological disorders, as they have been termed, can be brought about by great fluctuations in the temperature as when, for instance, plants are brought straight from a heated greenhouse to much cooler conditions outside. When fuchsias have not been hardened off sufficiently the foliage will probably turn dark purple within a day or so but although the plant has had a great shock it will usually make a good recovery when the new shoots appear. This will curtail the flowering for a time so it is far better to go to the trouble of seeing that hardening is done in stages.

Damage can also be brought about by the over-generous use of fertilisers; the roots suffer when this happens but the first signs are yellow or blotchy leaves with dark green veining. When only slightly affected the mere fact that the feeding is discontinued is normally enough to allow the plant to make a complete recovery. Should it still look anaemic after some weeks re-pot it into fresh compost.

Chemical sprays can cause severe scorching to tender foliage especially on some cultivars. As a precaution against this use only recommended materials at the correct strength. Spotting of foliage can also come about when plants are watered or remain wet in a sunny greenhouse, so see that they are watered in the late evening or early morning.

Appendix — the genus Fuchsia

Species of the genus *Fuchsia* arranged in their sections.
Key T=type plant   C=plants in cultivation in Britain (i.e. species usually offered for sale).
These are the species and subspecies of *Fuchsia* as revised by Dr Munz and Dr Breedlove.

1 Quelusia
campos-porti
bracelinae
magellanica var. *magellanica* T
         var. *macrostema* C
         var. *molinae* C
coccinea
regia var. *regia*
   var. *affinis*
   var. *alpestris* C
   var. *radicans*

2 Eufuchsia
abrupta
andrei
asperifolia
aspiazui
asplundii

austromontana
ayavacensis
boliviana var. *boliviana*
      var. *puberulenta*
      var. *luxurians* C
canescens
confertifolia
cordifolia
corymbiflora
cuatrecasasii
decussata
denticulata (serratifolia) C
fischeri
fulgens C
furfuracea
gehrigeri
glaberrima
hartwegii

81

hirtella
hypoleuca
jahnii
killipii
lehmannii
leptopoda
llewelynii
loxensis
macrophylla
macrostigma var. *macrostigma*
                var. *longiflora*
magdalinae
mathewsii
munzii
osgoodii
ovalis
pallescens
petiolaris var. *petiolaris*
              var. *bolivarensis*
pilosa
platypetala
polyantha
pringsheimii
putumayensis
rivularis
sanctae-rosae C
scabriuscula
sessilifolia
simplicicaulis C
smithii
splendens C
storkii
sylvatica
tincta
townshendii
triphylla T C

venusta var. *venusta*
            var. *huilensis*
verrucosa
woytkowskii

3 Kierschlegeria
lycioides

4 Skinnera
colensoi
cyrtandroides
excorticata T C
perscandens
procumbens C

5 Hemsleyella
apetala T
cestroides
decidua
garleppiana
hirsuta
juntasensis
macrantha
membranacea
salicifolia
tuberosa var. *tuberosa*
            var. *inflata*
tunariensis
unduavensis

6 Schufia
arborescens var. *arborescens* T C
                var. *tenuis*
                var. *parva*

7 Encliandra

microphylla var. *microphylla* C
        var. *hidalgensis*
        var. *quercetorum*
        var. *aprica*
        var. *hemsleyana*
thymifolia var. *thymifolia* C
        var. *minimaeflora* C

encliandra var. *encliandra* T
        var. *tetradactyla*
obconica
parviflora
ravenii
x bacillaris

Select Bibliography

Ewart, Ron, *Fuchsia Lexicon*, Blandford Press 1982
Goulding, E.J., *Fuchsias*, Bartholomew 1973
Munz, Dr Philip A., *A Revision of the Genus Fuchsia (Onagraceae)*, California Academy of Sciences 1943
Proudley, Brian and Valerie, *Fuchsias in Colour*, Blandford Press 1975
Puttock, A.G., *Lovely Fuchsias*, John Gifford 1959
Saunders, Eileen, *Wagtail's Book of Fuchsias*, Wagtail's Publications, Vol. I 1971, Vol. II 1972, Vol. III 1973
Travis, James, *Fuchsia Culture*, Travis
Wells, George, *Fuchsias*, Royal Horticultural Society 1972
Wilson, Stanley J., *Fuchsias*, Faber and Faber 1965

Glossary

Gardening and botanical terms used in the book.

ANTHER The swollen part at the end of the filament containing the pollen.

AXIL The angle between stem and leaf from which new shoots or flowers spring.

BERRY The fleshy fruit.

BREAK To branch, send out new growth from dormant wood.

CALYX Sepals and tube together, the outer part of the flower.

COMPOST (1) Correctly formulated garden soil used for potting.

COMPOST (2) Correctly rotted down garden refuse etc. A valuable source of humus.

COROLLA Collective term for the petals.

CULTIVAR Often abbreviated to cv or cvs (plural), this is the internationally accepted title for a 'man-made' garden plant.

FILAMENT The stalk of a stamen.

HYPANTHIUM *see* Tube.

INFLORESCENCE The complete flower.

MUTATE *see* Sport.

NODE Leaf-joints on a shoot, usually slightly swollen.

OVARY The part that contains the ovules which, after fertilisation, become the seeds. The ovary then swells to become a berry.

PEDICEL The flower-stalk.

PETAL One of the floral 'leaves' which together make up the corolla.

PETALOID A part of the flower which becomes petal-like in form, usually a stamen which develops a tiny petal-like appendage. Sometimes also used to describe the outer, reduced petals of the double corolla.

POT-BACK Re-pot a plant into a smaller sized pot than the one used the previous season.

PETIOLE Leaf-stalk.

POT-ON Re-pot a plant into a larger sized pot.

SEPAL(S) Together with the tube form the calyx.

SPORT A bud mutation which very often gives rise to a new cultivar.

STAMEN Filament and anther together, the male portion of the flower.

STIGMA The top of the style which being sticky allows pollen grains falling on it to adhere.

STOP Take out the growing tip.

STYLE The stalk which carries the stigma, together with the ovary forming the female part of the flower.

TUBE Correctly known as the hypanthium, it is the elongated part of the calyx. The tube and ovary are joined until the flower fades.

Principal Fuchsia Societies

Australia
Australian Fuchsia Society
Box No. 97
P.O. Norwood
South Australia 5067

Canada
British Columbia Fuchsia Society
2175 West 16th Avenue
Vancouver 9
British Columbia

Denmark
Secretariat v/Merete Printz
Frugtparken 1
2820 Gentofte

Ethiopia
Horticultural Society of Ethiopia
P.O. Box No. 1261
Addis Ababa

Germany
Deutsche Dahlien und Gladiolen Gesellschaft
674 Landau i d Pfalz
Den Altes Stadhaus
Koln

Great Britain
The British Fuchsia Society
29 Princes Crescent
Dollar
Clackmannanshire
FK14 6BW

Holland
Nederlandse Kring van Fuchsia Vrienden
Oranje Nassaulaan 32
Bilthoven
The Hague

New Zealand
Canterbury Horticultural Society
Fuchsia Circle
25 Albert Terrace
St. Martins
Christchurch 2

New Zealand Fuchsia Society
P.O. Box 8843
Symonds Street
Auckland 1

South Africa
South African Fuchsia Society
7 Maud Avenue
Scottsville 3201
Natal

United States of America
American Fuchsia Society
Hall of Flowers
Garden Center of San Francisco
Golden Gate Park
San Francisco
California 94122

National Fuchsia Society
6121 Monero Drive
Rancho Palos Verdes
California 90274

Zimbabwe
Fuchsia Society of Zimbabwe
P.O. Box GD 115
Greendale
Harare

Index

93